Understanding

BODY LANGUAGE

51 gestures and what they signal

ANTONI LACINAI

© 2016 Antoni Lacinai
Understanding Body Language – 51 gestures and what they signal
Art work: Pia Lilenthal
Illustrations: Antoni Lacinai
Photographer: Serny Pernebjer
Publisher: BoD
ISBN: 978-91-76991-84-8

You cannot *NOT* communicate

Whether you open your mouth or not, you communicate.

This guide provides you with 51 gestures and what they signal, consciously or unconsciously. According to communication experts at "The Center for Body Language" in Belgium, there is an 80% chance that these gestures correspond to different feelings. Still, you must look at:

- **The Context.** If you know that someone has just won the lottery or has been laid off, it helps you to interpret their gestures better.

- Possible **changes** from their **"base-line" behavior.** If a person with a normally open body language all of a sudden becomes closed off, it is a clear giveaway.

- Understanding when and how **several gestures** are used simultaneously or in succession can improve your interpretation of the message.

Toghether, these observations will give you a higher accuracy in your interpretations.

Next time you have a meeting, or sipping a coffee at a café, observe peoples' body language. Bring this book as a guide. Become an **emotional reader.**

Let's dive into the gestures!

Content

The Hands Communicate

The Legs Communicate

The Face Communicates

The Rest of the Body Communicates

The Hands Communicate

1. If you have your **palms up**, you show **openness** and **vulnerability**.

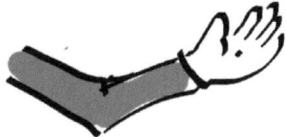

2. If you have your **palms down**, you show **dominance** and **authority.**

3. If you have your hands in your pockets like this, you signal **dominance.**

4. But if your hands are in your pockets like this, you make a **weak impression.**

5. Unless you spread your fingers like this, which is a mating signal = **Flirty.**

6. If you **point** at somebody with your **index finger** you signal **aggression.**

7. If you use your **thumb** to point, you show a **lack of respect.**

8. And if you point with your **whole arm**, you signal **control.**

9. If your **handshake** is **weak,** you seem **weak** and **unreliable.**

10. If you shake hands with your **palm** facing slightly **down**, you want to **dominate.**

11. While if your **palm** is facing slightly **up**, you seem **submissive** or **vulnerable.**

12. If your handshake is painfully **hard**, you come across as **aggressive.**

13. If you want to be in **control**, you **squeeze** the hand **10% harder** than your "opponent".

14. If your hands form a **pyramid,** you signal **confidence.**

15. If you **touch** the tip of your **nose**, you might **not** be telling the whole **truth.**

16. If you **scratch** the side of your **nose**, you may be a bit **angry** (unless you just have an itch of course).

17. If you **cover** your mouth when you speak, you don't **believe** what you **say,** or **see**.

8. If your **hands tremble**, you are probably **nervous.**

19. If you show your palms and **wrists openly**, you signal **comfort** and **safety.**

20. If you are **rubbing** your **hands** together, like when you are washing them in front of your body, you seem **excited** and **nervous.**

21. If you **rub** your **forehead** or touch your face gently, you feel **uneasy** and want to comfort yourself.

22. If you **rub** your **eyes**, you don't want to "see" the truth. You **disagree.**

23 If you **scratch** your **neck** during a conversation, you probably **disagree.**

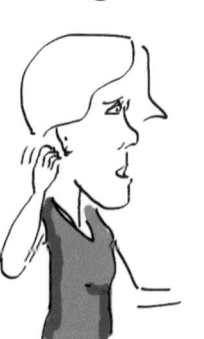

The Legs Communicate

24. If you stand with your **feet wide apart**, you show **dominance.**

25. If your stand with your **legs crossed** like this, you display **safety.**

26. If two people look like this, they feel **safe** in each other's company. They **mirror** each other by imitating each other's gestures.

27. If you **rub** your hands on your **thighs**, you seem **anxious.**

28. If you are **sitting down** and put your **hands** on your **knees**, it signals that you are ready to **leave.**

29. Feet pointing toward the **exit** could mean that you want to **leave.**

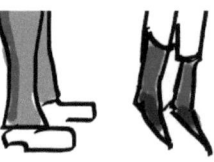

30. If you display this behavior, you are probably **upbeat.**

31. If you put your **hands to the side** with **thumbs** pointing **backward** (like a police officer) you show **dominance.** Contrarily, if your thumbs are pointing **forward**, you signal **weakness.**

The Face Communicates

32. An **asymmetric** smile signals **arrogance.**

33. A **symmetrical** smile is a more genuine sign of **happiness**, especially combined with **wrinkles** in your eyes.

34. If your **eyebrows** look like this, you are probably **sad.**

35. And even more so if it is combined with a raised lower lip.

36. This on the other hand, signals **anger** – or possibly **concentration.**

37. And if your **lips** are also **pressed** hard together, you are most probably **pissed off.**

38. If your **upper lip** goes up like this, and your **nose wrinkles**, you feel **disgust.**

39. With **high eyebrows** and your **jaw dropped,** you signal **surprise.**

40. High eyebrows combined with a **stiff, broad mouth** signals **fear.**

41. People under **pressure** or **stress** sometimes **purse** their **lips** shortly and then release them.

42. If you **pout** your **lips**, you might **disagree** (or perhaps you are getting ready for a selfie).

The Rest of the Body Communicates

43. If you all of a sudden look like a **turtle**, your **confidence** is **gone.**

44. If your **upper body leans away** from the other person, you feel **uncomfortable.**

45. If you sit heavily **leaned back** in a chair, you signal that you **aren't** taking the situation **seriously.**

46. If you look like this, you display **vulnerability.** This is not a sign of weakness since you show that you don't feel threatened.

47. If you try to **"get more air"** you feel **bad** and want to calm down.

48. Putting your hand on your chin like this = **Bored.**

49. If you look like this, you show both **self confidence** and **dominance.**

50. When your **nose** goes **up**, so does your a**rrogance, pride** and **superiority.**

51. If you have an open body language, and all of a sudden do this, it could mean that you are getting into something **sensitive,** especially if you squeeze hard.

Final Notes

I hope that you've already started to observe your surroundings with new eyes, and that you're having fun doing it. Remember to focus on your own behavior too. You cannot not communicate. Build your toolbox with gestures that show your authenticity. Do it right and people will have an easier time understanding you.

As you might have noticed, I have chosen to present the gestures starting from the head and then moving down the body. There are other ways of presenting clues to peoples' body language and when I give lectures I normally use another approach. Let me end this guide by explaining body language from this perspective.

You can divide many gestures into the following three categories:
- **Vulnerable** gestures
- **Uncomfortable** gestures
- **Dominant** and **arrogant** gestures.

You demonstrate your **vulnerability** and **comfort** if you have an open body language, exposing your torso, wrists and neck. The same applies if you have an imbalanced pose or look away from time to time. You can see this in points 11, 25 and 46 above.

You signal **discomfort** if you clutch your hands in front of your torso, if you stroke your arms or legs, or if you point your body to the exit. Examples of this are illustrated in cases 21, 27 and 44.

You come across as **dominant** or **arrogant** if you exaggerate comfort gestures or use power poses. Examples of this are illustrated in cases 7, 31 and 50.

Ask yourself the following questions regarding your own body language:

- Do they match the image of how I would like to be described?
- Do they match the feeling I want to convey?
- What can I do to strengthen or clarify my communication?

There are tons of books on body language to read. Two of my favorites are Joe Navarro's *What Everybody Is Saying*, and Paul Ekman's *Emotions revealed.*

I wish you the best of luck in your quest to become an emotional reader!

//Antoni Lacinai

Antoni Lacinai is an international public speaker and communication skills trainer. He is an author of several books on communication and goal setting. His own communication style is a mix of high energy, empathy and clarity.

Although based in Sweden, his lectures, trainings and books have influenced people around the world to enhance their communication skills when leading, cooperating, presenting, selling or setting motivating goals.

Find out more at www.lacinai/about-antoni-lacinai where you also have contact details to Antoni.

Printing: BoD – Books on Demand, Stockholm, Sweden
Production: BoD – Books on Demand, Norderstedt, Germany